PRAISE

Joe's American Life is quite a contrast to Ronald Reagan's autobiography, *An American Life.* I can recommend both readings without reservation. I am proud to say Joe Ostrenger was my friend.

—Donald L.Fife

WIN SOME | LOSE SOME

the MOTHER LODE

JANE J. DELVEAUX

WIN SOME | LOSE SOME

the MOTHER LODE

Tate Publishing & *Enterprises*

Published by Tate Publishing & Enterprises, LLC
127 E. Trade Center Terrace | Mustang, Oklahoma 73064 USA
1.888.361.9473 | www.tatepublishing.com

Tate Publishing is committed to excellence in the publishing industry. The company reflects the philosophy established by the founders, based on Psalm 68:11,
"The Lord gave the word and great was the company of those who published it."

Cover design by Kellie Southerland
Interior design by Jeff Fisher

Published in the United States of America

ISBN: 978-1-61663-022-5
Biography & Autobiography, Adventurers & Explorers
10.04.01

DEDICATION

Dedicated to the memory of Joe Ostringer in recognition of the life fully spent on audacious acts of discovery. Though oft accompanied by outrageous mischief, he finished the race well.

Dedicated to the family members who are running their own race today and members who have yet to begin. May they finish so well that they may say, "I have fought a good fight. I have finished my course. I have kept the faith" (2 Timothy 4:7 KJV).

> Henceforth there is laid up for me a crown of righteousness, which the Lord, the righteous judge, shall give me at that day; and not to me only, but unto all them also that love his appearing.
>
> 2 Timothy 4:8 (KJV)

ACKNOWLEDGMENTS

Stories are based on conversations between Joe Ostringer and the author. Research relies heavily on the few written notes taken over the years. Not all details are verifiable.

Attempts to unravel the stories were somewhat successful. Valuable information was obtained from newspaper articles, a TV documentary, a photo copy of a signed contract, books, public records, photographs, and Web sites.

Special thanks to Donald L. Fife, CPG, for his public service and patriotism, for the support that he has shown to miners in their fight for the protection of land rights, for the personal support he offered Joe Ostringer, and for his kind response to this writer's request for information that would aid in understanding the disposition of Joe's wollastonite mine.

More thanks to this writer's firstborn, Laurie (Delveaux) Parisey, for the technical support that put pictures and supportive documents to these pages. It was her encouragement that changed what seemed impossible to what became possible and it was the generous positive comments from the rest of the family that caused the stories to come to life.

Early impetus for this project came from great niece, Laura Lederer, who years ago pleaded, "Tell me about Uncle Joe".

> Take notes on the spot, a note is worth a cartload of recollections.
>
> —Ralph Waldo Emerson

TABLE OF CONTENTS

FOREWORD

Non-Conformist Leads His Own War Against the Establishment

Separating truth from fiction proved to be a challenge during the process of collecting stories from miner-geologist Joe Ostringer. On the face of it and without further investigation, he could have only been described as eccentric. Who would believe that he led a life as footloose and unconventional as Indiana Jones. From bootlegging in the Midwest; to panning for gold in Colorado; to finding treasure in the Yucatan; to worldwide travels and adventures; to daredevil escapades in the West; to business ventures; to prospecting, mining, and eventually finding the mother lode, this adventurer had more stories than he could remember to tell.

At first, collecting stories from an *old timer* was out of curiosity and without any idea that they were really *collectables.* Discovering that his strange experiences eventually led him to, singlehandedly, take on the U.S. Dept. of Interior, U.S. Attorney General, Janet Reno, and Secretary of the U.S. Dept. of Interior, Bruce Babbitt, in the nation's highest courts, changed the way that I looked at the man.

Joe was a singularly unusual uncle with strongly rebellious ideas. To those of us from the Midwest, he had the most unorthodox lifestyle we had ever seen. It was marked with a deeply embedded distrust of all government agencies. He held a belief that there was a conspiracy, within the government, for the invasion of personal privacy and for the control of personal and public property.

This man had rejected what the rest of us consider normal lifestyles, our very civilization, for a life of combing the deserts and mountains. Although he enjoyed modern conveniences and luxurious living, he traded that all in, time and again, for his first passion: the pursuit of treasure.

The pursuit took him around the world. He had a deep fascination for mineralogy and after his earlier years of mischief, adventures, and misadventures, he spent the rest of his life as a miner and self-taught geologist. The culmination of a lifetime of searching ended in the discovery of the world's largest deposit of the mineral—wollestonite, a deposit considered priceless. He had found his treasure.

The Indiana Jones part of his life was over, and he had embarked on the development of what was described as a world-class mine by preeminent geologists in both hemispheres. However, the true grit of this miner was tested by the full onslaught of the environmentalists and the federal government in their war on the West. The outcome of his battle reveals the awful invasion and disposition of personal and property rights that has taken place in our country; reveals the high cost of opposing government and non-government agencies; and reveals what a *win* means when these agencies are challenged.

Information on the machinations of environmentalists groups to confiscate and take control of this nation's most valuable lands has been condensed into a book of short stories designed to catch the attention of U.S. citizens who choose to reject long-winded rhetoric. The entertainment value is designed to draw in the general public who will appreciate the audacity of the character. The legal battle waged by this miner will catch the attention of individual miners as well as miners' unions in the West, especially in Nevada, who may find themselves reeling under continuous government intrusions.

This work is written in layman's terms in order to impress the many who have chosen to be observers that there is a need for active participation in the democratic process if there is to be any hope in preserving individual rights and defending our republic. The price of an I-don't-care attitude and the cost of inaction may be higher than what we, living in what used to be the land of opportunity, are willing to pay. The stories are also meant to further information in the archives of those who continue the battle.

This book catches glimpses of the imaginative escapades and sometimes illegal activities of an individual who turned his life into a campaign for individual freedom, from outlaw to hero.

INTRODUCTION

Newspaper accounts say that he followed the path of the trailblazers and Forty-Niners. The eldest of eleven children, he was born in Birch Creek, Michigan. His father, (Michal) Michael Ostrenga, had emigrated from Poland, the state of Kradow, Poviat (or county of) Tarnow, Village of Smigno in the 1890s. His mother, Louise Kolodziej, was also born in Poland. Other children born to this immigrant couple were Walter, Edward, Julie, John, Frank, Martin, Louise, George, Stanley, and Raymond.

This firstborn son's given name was Joseph, which in Hebrew means *May God give increase.* The name proved to be a good choice for an adventurous boy who would grow up to be a mischievous treasure seeker.

It was in 1924 that Joe began to exhibit his independent, rebellious nature. At the greatly advanced age of fourteen, he left the family farm in Oconto Falls, Wisconsin, where his family then resided. Farming was not the life for him, and he would have no more of it. He was off for the big cities of Milwaukee and Chicago, with grand ideas, to begin his life as an adventurer.

Fortunately for Joe, he had good resources that he could call on. Five of his dad's brothers were well established in Milwaukee and were able to help him locate housing and a job. By the time he was sixteen, it seemed he had earned enough money to buy a car. Now, there would be no more stopping him.

> A farm is a hunk of land on which, if you get up early enough mornings and work late enough nights, you'll make a fortune—if you strike oil on it.
>
> —"Fibber" McGee (Jim Jordan)

Leaving his short past behind him, Joe headed west. He was on his way to becoming the perpetual speculator, wanderer, and fearless prospector and miner who would one day take on the full power of the Federal Government in a costly legal battle that lasted more than nine years.

Travel, in those days, was over unpaved roads. Whether by design or not, the roads led him to the gold fields of Cripple Creek. Colorado was still a favorite destination for other wanderers with gold-fever who were seeking to make their fortunes.

Panning for gold was slow, hard work, but Joe decided to give it a try. There were no frills or comforts of home, just a blanket on the ground. Stubbornness and hard labor produced enough gold to finance the rest of his trip to California. It also introduced him to a way of life that became a series of adventures and misadventures that rival anything done by the fictitious Indiana Jones.

In the 1990s, when I first began to ask Joe to share stories about his life, he needed little prodding. His home was now in Pahrump, Nevada, and close to some of his most significant mine holdings.

Pahrump is a community located in the heart of Nevada's pioneer territory called The Solitudes. This is an area that contains some of the country's most beautiful desert vistas. Pahrump is considered the Gateway to Death Valley where a person can see Mother Nature in the raw. It is less than an hour's drive away from Las Vegas. Both cities, located in deep, long valleys between mountain ranges, are growing at a rate that makes it all but impossible to maintain an accurate census.

Joe was my father's brother, and it had become my mission to bring these brothers together in their declining years. The trip from Wisconsin to Nevada became an annual event. Each year I collected a few more stories. But, Joe admitted that his recall of his early years was beginning to fade. Many names and dates had long been forgotten. Though details were often missing, just listening to the telling was awesome. There were so many incredible stories that I was left with the question of whether they just might be imaginings and half-truths. I wanted to get to know more about this mysterious man.

We were sitting in his living room one afternoon in 1996 when the phone rang. The phone conversation that I heard was one-sided. But, I overheard Joe tell the caller, "Under no circumstances would I ever consider doing that again … If I remembered how to get there, which I don't, it would be way too dangerous.

It was a foolish thing to do then, and I'm not foolish enough to do it again. No, I want to live longer..." Joe was surprised by the call but was happy to talk about it.

1

The Stories Begin

TO THE YUCATAN AND BACK

> We are told that talent creates its own opportunities. But it sometimes seems that intense desire creates not only its own opportunities, but its own talents.
>
> —Eric Hoffer

Joe had, for many years, been telling close family members of a reckless voyage that he had taken to the Yucatan while he was still in his teens. Of all his stories, this one had to be over the top.

It seems that Joe had become acquainted with two other rebellious boys soon after arriving in California.

These boys were all about the same age and more than a little foolhardy. Envision this footloose crew partying, plotting, and planning mischief together, slugging down cheap moonshine with glowing cigarettes hanging out of their mouths.

Together, they concocted a get-rich scheme. They would outfit a boat, take it down the Gulf Coast, and set a course for the unexplored jungles of the Yucatan where they intended to search for treasure.

Not to be daunted by petty details, Joe and friends faced their biggest challenge and searched for a seaworthy boat. They decided on a gunboat. How they were able to come up with a gunboat is a mystery. Collecting basic supplies was the easy part, and these new seamen were soon underway on their journey into the unknown.

As this group of highly inexperienced sailors began their questionable expedition through the Gulf of Mexico, there were no treasure maps to follow. They were guided by their youthful energy, wishful thinking, and unseen guardian angels of whose presence they were totally unaware. The weather was favorable, and the clear blue waters were calm. When they tired of sailing and found a likely beaching area, they anchored the boat securely and set ashore.

The sailors now became hikers. Packing everything they needed on their lean backs and guided by only a simple compass, they set off stumbling into the hot, humid interior with the spirit of hopeful pioneers.

The dense jungle was a tangle of tropical vegetation and trees. For a week, they moved through this wild, uninhabited part of the country by cutting paths for themselves with machetes. It was hot, sweaty work, but they reveled in it.

Survival in the jungle meant sleeping in trees to keep away from snakes and animals; covering with netting to keep mosquitoes away; gathering drinking water using palm leaves; and eating fruit from the trees. They were intruders on this lush landscape that seemed so undisturbed by human habitation, and they ran into many strange animals, including screaming monkeys. This didn't look anything like home. Each step was a challenge. Joe recalled, "All of us were youngsters. None of us had any brains. No one was scared."

As the story goes, the search was haphazard. Joe said that it was "by pure dumb luck" that found the hikers practically tripping over a massive stone structure that was hidden by heavy growths of roots and vines. Standing together, they enjoyed the wonder of their discovery. To them, it looked like the remains of an ancient pyramid. They were determined to find out if the structure contained anything of value and proceeded to cut their way inside as if their lives depended on it.

After these would-be explorers had succeeded in gaining access, they could not believe their good fortune. In Las Vegas terms, they had hit the jackpot, and it stood wide open before them. No pot of gold could have looked grander to their greedy eyes.

This would be the point where the jumping, the whooping, the hollering, and celebrating took place. Any ordinary, sensible adult would have known this find was impossible. Yet there it was: a treasury of gold and silver and, best of all, jewelry. Three sets of incredulous eyes fastened on the cache of jewelry set with precious gems of all sorts. It was all laid out before them on rock shelves along the walls.

Because the boys were on foot, they faced a major dilemma. They could see there was too much to carry, and they had to choose what to take. It was decided that the gold and silver items were too heavy and bulky and these items had to be left behind. The gems were an easy choice because of their intrinsic value and because they would be the lightest to transport.

Joe made a point of adding that they also "found corpses." Apparently they were spooked by that sight because they left the corpses alone and did not remove any jewelry that the corpses had on them. Laden with all that they could carry, it was an excited group that backtracked along the original machete-hacked trail.

Despite the now much heavier load in their backpacks, the struggles that the bearers of newfound treasure encountered coming out must have seemed much lighter than the struggles encountered when they had first entered the jungle. They were soon back on their boat with their find and not as much as a scratch or a stubbed toe.

During the return trip to Galveston, the realization of the enormity of what they had just done began to set in and overcame some of their excitement. The voyage had been successful, but they realized that they had completed an unlawful expedition. Whether or not any one of them felt even a slight twinge of guilt or even nervousness, it was evident that none of them wanted their deed to be discovered.

Before setting foot on shore, they made a pact as they divided the jewelry between all three. They shook hands, and they swore to never reveal each others' names and to never contact each other again. According to the plan they had agreed on, they left in different directions. Joe said, "In fifteen minutes, we were all off the boat and got lost."

The pact remained unbroken until the afternoon, in 1996, when Joe's phone rang and the caller spoke to Joe about returning to the place where they had left so much treasure behind. Being a witness to one side of the call on that day gave me pause to consider the truth of the Yucatan story.

The Yucatan peninsula has vast areas of unexplored tropical rainforests. By the year 2007, *five-thousand structures, that often have the features of temple-tomb or pyramid-palaces, had been excavated and mapped. Ruins were not excavated in the area of the popular tourist attraction of Belize until* 1974. *Teams of archeologists continue their search and add to the number of discoveries regularly. See Web site.*

2

BUYING AND SELLING GEMS

Next to good judgment, diamonds and pearls are the rarest things in the world.

—Jean De La Bruyere

How much a dunce that has been sent to roam, excels a dunce that has been kept at home.

—William Cowper

Converting gems to cash was a learning process for Joe. These were ill-gotten gains, and he realized that he had to be careful. Joe said, "At first, I'd hock the pieces one at a time. After I got wise to the value, I went to antique dealers. I'd dress all up in a suit, like I was wealthy." This worked so well that Joe was able to live the life of the idle rich for quite an extended period of time. He took his leisure in deciding what to do next.

This was a *win-some* part of Joe's life. Things were looking up, especially from behind the wheel of his shiny new Duisenberg automobile. During this period and sporadically over the years that followed, Joe was a traveler. The world became his school. His formal education had never gotten much beyond elementary school, but he had a hunger for learning and spent a good deal of time reading and studying. His major interests were in mining and geology. Never one to do things halfway, he taught himself out in the field. This is where he lost his heart to the West.

Before the *lose-some* time came when Joe's first fortune would be gone, he was figuring out new ways to make another million. The life of leisure would be over when the gems were gone.

The building of Hoover Dam (Boulder Dam) in the early 1930s had proven to be a solid source of income for Joe, as he must have found that he was running low on jewels and money. From now on, he would be no stranger to dangerous, hard, sweaty work. It would be what energized him and drove him on.

The nearness of the Hoover Dam project to the California and Nevada deserts and mountains, but especially the nearness to the Las Vegas casinos, led Joe to decide to take on the offer of work as a laborer. He survived and thrived on the harsh environment and poor living conditions, while accidents and disease claimed the lives of many other good men.

One would think that the *win-some* part of Joe's life was over by 1937 when he was prompted to make a return trip to visit his family in Wisconsin. The car he was driving had been in an accident, yet he was able to coax it along miles of death-defying, rugged desert and mountain roads as it limped its way back to Milwaukee.

At the family re-union, there was the usual celebration, which included a good deal of heavy partying, before Joe dropped his grand plan on his brother, Walter. There is no doubt that Joe could be a conniver. By nature, he was jovial and could be totally disarming. This always made it easy for him to *make friends and influence people.* Despite the fact that Walter had a family of his own to support, Joe used all of his best skills to convince Walter to co-sign for a car loan. It didn't take long for him to disappear into the sunset, leaving the city on squealing wheels and in a cloud of dust.

After Joe returned to California, it was a couple of years before he was heard from again. Walter and his wife, Margaret, were left to be *on foot* for that first year while they paid off Joe's loan.

On the other hand, by the end of the 1930s some of Joe's diggings were paying off and he was somehow able to come up with enough money to purchase an outstanding business property in Baker, California. This would not be the only time that Joe would get so caught up in his own world that his brothers were left *holding the bag.*

The car loan had long since been forgiven when Joe guided his brother, Walter, and this writer to that mountainous area, years later. Hoover Dam was included in this tour. It was there that he proudly pointed to the blasted mountain walls and the immense cement structure that made up Hoover Dam. He spoke of how dynamite was used, how it was placed, its dangers, and its powerful effects. He told of the way cement was mixed, how it was poured, how dangerous the job was, and how quickly the cement set.

During this tour, Walter pointed out that, from his hometown, he had actively contributed to Hoover Dam, also. The building of the dam's 13,800 *volt generator took place at the West Allis (Milwaukee) Allis Chalmers works where he was employed as a pattern maker. That plant supplied seven of the eleven hydraulic turbine units along with the generators and switchgear.*

One will never know how many states or how many continents Joe had crossed in any given year. In all of his pursuits, he was undaunted by distance and time. Sandwiched into his life, as an up and coming prospector, he made sure to pursue adventures. A brilliant gem played a major part of one of his best remembered experiences.

Some time while Stalin was still in power, Joe made a trip to Russia. It may have been financed with money obtained from the sale of the gems, but more probably took place several years later. It would have been before 1953, but it is hard to know exactly when this was done. Whatever the period, he was especially proud of the ride he took on the Trans-Siberian Railroad.

From 1916 *through* 1984, *the railroad was the only thoroughfare across the entirety of Siberia.* In his later years, Joe claimed to have visited every major continent. Despite extensive travels, he thought of the train ride as a special feat.

It was on this trip that he found a Russian peasant jeweler who had a prize Alexandrite stone the size of a grape. Joe had become quite savvy about gems, albeit surreptitiously. He became enamored with the utter size and color of this stone and bargained long and hard to convince the peasant to sell it to him.

If there was a question whether Joe had really traveled as much as he claimed, the sight of the Alexandrite stone lent a certain amount of credibility to his claims. He always wore a ring on his finger that held a rich-colored Alexandrite stone in a heavy silver-setting, which he had made himself. Transforming himself into a jeweler, he fashioned the silver in the ring from silver that was extracted from the ore from one of his mines. In 1996, it had been worn for so long that the stone was in its third setting.

After the Yucatan, and during the time that he was working again, Joe continued to take extended trips into the mountains and deserts of the West His wanderings were only beginning and led to experiences that made good stories. It is known that over the years that followed, he laid claim and recorded over two-hundred mines in Colorado, Nevada, and California.

3

INDIAN GEORGE AND THE WELLS FARGO BUCKLE

Poverty sits by the cradle of all our great men and rocks all of them to manhood.

—Heinrich Heine

When asked by an anthropologist what the Indians called America before the white man came, an Indian said simply, "Ours."

—Vine Deloria, Jr.

In 1996, Joe's trailer home in Pahrump, Nevada, was the resting place of an unusual assortment of *things*. What he had valued the most is what he had kept.

One day on one of my visits, an odd-shaped, metal object, about the size of the palm of a man's hand, caught my attention. Joe picked it up and turned it over to show me an inscription written on the back. It looked something like this: *Made by Tiffany. Property of Wells Fargo. Reward offered for return.*

Obviously, the reward was never collected since the *property* was still in Joe's house. I was told that this was a belt buckle. It had been artistically crafted with the face showing a horse-drawn stagecoach. The Wells Fargo buckle had a long and unexpected story attached to it.

On one of Joe's frequent expeditions, he had climbed and was atop a rocky ledge in what probably would have been the Panamint Mountain Range. He had been prospecting and mining in the area. This spot offered a panoramic view of the valley below and had very limited access. The lay of the land caused him to remember an interesting Indian legend about an outlaw band that had roamed the area robbing stagecoaches.

Sometime earlier while in the area, Joe had made a stop at an Indian reservation near Death Valley. He was told the story about a *renegade* outlaw leader by the name of Indian George. This aged outlaw was still living on the reservation. It was said that he and his elusive band of stagecoach robbers had been active in the very late 1800s. Their success was more related to their survival than any loot that they had gotten. Joe knew that Indian George lived to be more than one hundred years old.

The storytellers on the reservation pointed to a mountain where it was said that the renegade band could watch the road through a crevice. It was also said by the story-tellers that the outlaws were really only interested in the horses and consumable goods. Horses, taken from an enemy, would have been especially considered as prize trophies. Whatever else they had gotten was discarded.

While standing on the ledge, Joe began to wonder if he was near the place where the band would hide after a robbery. It was in the general area that had been pointed out. It also seemed like an ideal location that matched some of the other descriptions that he had heard.

Being a man always in search of treasure, he spent the next days looking and digging into rocks and crevices. His curiosity had been peaked by the drama of stagecoach holdups, the last vestiges of Indian resistance to government relocations. The possibility that the Indian raiders had escaped with white man's valuables gave Joe all the reason he needed to embark on a search of his own. According to his rationale, there should be a hole or holes where the robbers would have dumped what they couldn't use.

Joe claimed that, during his search, he found a crevice that looked so promising that he brought some of his equipment to the spot. There was no way to dig to the bottom because of its extreme depth. But, mining was his business and he knew another way to get to the bottom by taking a small detour. Using an air jackhammer, he began drilling underneath the crevice into what proved to be a successful dig.

The results were worth the effort and just what Joe had hoped for. The outlaws had been good at their job and had gotten away with a lot more loot than just horses. They had kept what they wanted and left the rest behind. At the bottom of the crevice, he found that they had dropped heavy, *useless* objects like the Wells Fargo belt buckle and gold coins.

Just like retrieving sunken treasure in the ocean, Joe felt justified in retrieving the contents of the dig and keeping these things for himself. Selling the coins slowly over several years netted him about $40,000 and provided the stakes for more exploring. But, he kept the belt buckle. It was the one treasure that didn't get away.

Searching into the Nevada historical archives for any record of these outlaws, in 2008, *proved to be disappointing. The state is full of Boot Hills with markers that show the early years were overrun by outlaw-type activities. Commentaries, about the Nevada archives, indicate that historical researchers have regrettably been unable to locate accurate information on many of the colorful figures that roamed and often ravaged the state.*

A visit to the Timbisha Shoshone reservation near Furnace Creek, Nevada, would be a place to go for anyone wanting more information. No doubt, Joe knew this area well. The Shoshone of the Panamint Valley were often referred to as Panamints. History has recorded a Panamint by the name of Indian George (b. 1841 *– d.* 1945*). It is believed that the oral history of this very small group contains a great deal of information about individual lives and uprisings that have never been recorded.*

4

THE SHAH OF IRAN AND THE MALACHITE TABLE

Every individual has a place to fill in the world and is important, in some respect, whether he chooses to be so or not.

—Nathaniel Hawthorne (1804–1864)

The story of the malachite table had its beginnings in Pahrump, Nevada, where I was first introduced to it. Although Joe had probably come into possession of this rare find shortly after his expedition to the Yucatan, no matter where he lived, the table went with him. It seemed that the dry desert air had been as kind to it as it had been to Joe. It was there, after more than half a century of wanderings, that it came to rest in a dilapidated storage shed, all but forgotten.

The table looked dusty and uncared for since, by now, Joe had been widowed for a few years and his fortunes had changed. Joe pointed to the table to tell me that the tabletop was made of malachite.

On a closer look, I could see a most beautiful forest green, heavy, two-inch-thick stone top. This solid block of Malachite was worth a man's small fortune. The curved woodwork and carved legs were covered with gold leaves, which only added to the value. I told Joe that I wanted to know the story of the table. It seems that Joe's table had a history, indeed.

From what I had seen, I knew that Joe was never shy. While still a relatively young man, and probably while he still was able to live extravagantly, he had become friends with a fellow who, at the time, was still living in San Clemente, California, with his wealthy parents.

The friend was one of six sons of Ole Hanson, a former mayor of Seattle, Washington. Although this mayor had been in office only a very brief time, he had restored economic stability to Seattle and achieved *hero* status by breaking a crippling strike.

After retirement from office, this mayor found investors and bought real estate south of Los Angeles with the intention of building a modern city. The city of San Clemente became an actuality in 1925. He called this growing community his *Spanish Community by the Sea* and called the new house that he had built *Casa Romantica.*

In his early years, Joe was often a guest in the Hanson home and Mayor Hanson had taken a liking to him. There were many things to admire in the home, but when Joe saw the Malachite stone on the table, he couldn't resist asking about it.

Mayor Hanson indicated that in 1919, during the time that he was mayor, he took a European tour and traveled to Iran where he met the shah. It is unknown if Mayor Hanson had a gift to present, but the shah nonetheless presented the table to the mayor.

The Malachite table had followed Mayor Hanson to Seattle and then to San Clemente where it rested and where Joe first saw it. Joe had an intense appreciation of minerals and mining which was obvious enough to prompt the mayor to immediately gift the table to Joe.

This would have happened circa 1930 *since the mayor lost his Casa Romantica during the Great Depression and died in* 1940.

I don't know how many homes the table actually had after that, but it must have traveled to several. According to Joe, the mayor's home was eventually sold to President Richard Nixon.

Joe believed that the shah's gift to the mayor, which he now possessed, had become priceless. At one time, it had been given a prominent place in Joe's San Fernando home, as can still be seen in photos that were taken.

Before being relegated to its poor resting place in a dry desert shed, Joe had offered and the table had been accepted for a temporary display in a museum, *possibly in Los Angeles,* where it was given its due respect.

See Web site, *A biography of Mayor Ole Hanson.*

5

A MAN, A MOUNTAIN, AND AN AIRPLANE

We must have courage to bet on our ideas,
to take the calculated risk, and to act.
Everyday living requires courage if life is to
be effective and bring happiness.

—Maxwell Maltz

Over the years, Joe had boasted of what has to be considered one of his most dangerous escapades. This episode lasted only a few hours but shows the daring makeup of a man who didn't give consideration to the consequences of his actions.

A day came when Joe was in high country, probably in California, visiting a friend. His friend owned a small airplane and invited Joe to go for a ride to see the lay of the land from the air. For someone who spent his life walking, climbing, and digging his way across California, Colorado, and Nevada, this would have been an offer he couldn't refuse.

They took off from a short runway that had been built on one of the hills and enjoyed the thrill of flight and the panoramic view of bright vistas and the valley below. This seems to have been Joe's first flight, and it must have been intoxicating. It was over too soon to suit Joe.

After his friend landed the plane and exited it, Joe impulsively got behind the stick. An idea started brewing in his mind. He either thought this would be a good joke or believed the Greek proverb, "No need to teach an eagle to fly."

Whatever the reason, instead of getting out, Joe put on full throttle and jolted down the runway for a take-off. I can imagine his friend waving his arms, shouting some very unprintable words, and running down the runway after Joe.

Joe always laughed in the telling, especially when describing the landing. Take-offs are no great trick in a small airplane, so he took the plane to cruising altitude without difficulty. This type of plane was designed to almost fly itself as long as it had enough speed.

The landing proved to be another story. A runway that is perched on a hill has an eloquent view of nothing but space when a plane is landing. Adding to the difficulty was the fact that the plane was a "taildragger." This meant that he had no forward visibility and could only see the landing strip by looking out the side windows as he tried to touch down. He didn't want the plane to drop out of the sky onto the runway, nor did he like the idea of dropping off the end of the runway. He said that he made so many botched landing attempts that he thought he must have been out of fuel and flying on fumes. He finally had to commit to setting down on the runway and held his breath.

Fortunately, although the landing was nothing to brag about, Joe didn't break much. He was able to walk away to face the man who probably wanted to take him down. Joe had a postscript to add. It had to do with the idea that his trousers may have undergone a color change.

6

CASINOS: MONEY IN, MONEY OUT

> Americans have mastered the art of being
> prosperous though broke.
>
> —Billy Boy Franklin

> Forty for you, sixty for me, and equal partners we will be.
>
> —Gerald Barzan

For almost seventy years of Joe's life, and throughout his many wanderings and ventures, the thrill of discovery was the motivator that led him down the path of miner. There were times when he was richer and times when he was poorer. It seemed that he had taken almost $3,000,000 worth of minerals out of some of the claims. He had sold the mineral rights of two mines in Colorado. One of the mines produced silver-rich ore. Not all of his profits went back into the ground. At those times, when he had money, he had a couple of other interesting business ventures.

He remembered a time when there were only five gambling casinos in Las Vegas. In the 1940s, a man by the name of Wilbur Clark ran out of cash and said he needed $50,000 to finish building what was then called the Wilbur Clark Desert Inn.

Joe had more than a few contacts in the West. One of them was a Los Angeles Realtor by the name of William Pauly Day. The two of them decided to try to raise the cash and loan it to Clark. Joe must have seen a profit to be made, and Clark could offer twelve or fourteen single dwelling apartments that he owned as security. However, it seemed that the would-be investors could not raise enough cash. In order to keep the Desert Inn, Clark decided to make a deal for the money with *mafioso* contacts in Chicago.

It was the Cleveland mob that Clark ended up doing business with. Since they did not trust Clark, they sent "Moe" Dolitz to Las Vegas to see the place before they gave him any money. The history of gangland investments, in this gambling town, is notorious. Wilbur Clark ended up being the public front man when "Moe" took over what became the infamous Desert Inn. It was eventually bought out by Howard Hughes.

Joe found that the excitement of gambling got into his blood. He was a frequent visitor and player in Nevada casinos. He could see this was a business where profits were being made, and he began to consider that being a casino owner might be a good business for himself.

Since it could be unhealthy to compete in Las Vegas, Joe decided to play it safe and find another location. With a little searching, he found a piece of property near Searchlight, Nevada. It was about fifty-five miles south of Las Vegas and suited his purpose.

Although this was just a little flicker of space in an unpopulated area, it was situated at the base of a small mountain from which it received rich mineral waters. The mineral springs brought visitors to the area. With high expectations, Joe built and put money into the Golden Nugget. He hired the dealers, and this enterprise was off to a good start.

That good start didn't last long. Joe decided that the role of businessman was not going to interfere with his prospecting, and he was soon off into the hills again. Leaving someone else in charge of the Golden Nugget while he was gone turned out to be a bad idea. When he returned, he found that the person in charge, along with the dealers, had "robbed him blind." He recalled that he would have sold the casino, but before this could happen, it was leveled by a tornado, and he was very sadly money-out.

Joe never lost his interest in casinos. Visits to Joe, in Pahrump, usually included visits to Las Vegas. He took great delight in showing his visitors from the Midwest the bright lights, the sights, and the shrimp cocktails. On one occasion, he ordered five cocktails for each one in our party. When we objected that we would never be able to eat that much, he laughed and said he could find someone, within two minutes, to eat what was left.

Just as we thought, we had to leave an entire tray of cocktails on the table. Without blinking, Joe got up and walked out the door. As he promised, he returned with two men in tow. He had recognized them as panhandlers. They took good care of the food, and Joe had a great laugh.

See Web site for Story of the Desert Inn.

7

THE BROTHERHOOD OF PROSPECTORS

Nothing splendid has ever been achieved except by those who dared believe that something inside them was superior to circumstances.

—Bruce Barton

A journalist accurately captured Joe's profile in a published Nevada newspaper article. The article colorfully described Joe by stating that Joe came to the Mojave Desert area near the close of the era of the greatest of the old-time prospectors. These were men like Shorty Harris, Seldom Seen Slim, One-eyed Thompson, and Death Valley Scotty. They were rugged men who had braved the California and Nevada wilderness areas. They were men who were driven by visions of finding such mineral-rich ores as gold, silver, and lead.

Joe fit the stereotype of these old-time prospectors to a tee and became identified as one of them. He had become just as grizzled, crusty, and sun-baked, and could probably cuss and drink with the best of them.

His frame was light and his body sinewy. He probably never weighed more than 140 pounds. He liked to brag that even with all of his smoking and drinking he could still out-work and out-hike any and all of the laborers that he had ever hired.

He spoke of a friendship that he had developed with Walter Scott, better known as, Scotty, *Death Valley Scotty.* Scotty's fame did not come from being a successful prospector because this is what he was not. He was a much better scam artist and had been selling interests in a phony gold mine.

Despite his bad behavior, Scotty had gotten in the graces of a good-humored insurance magnate from Chicago by the name of Albert Johnson. This gentleman decided he didn't care that there was no gold in the mine. He found Scotty to be an enjoyable companion.

Johnson loved the area around Grapevine Canyon so much that he wanted to build a comfortable place where he and his wife could stay on their visits. His idea of a comfortable place was especially grand for this part of the country. He had plans drawn, and he asked Scotty to oversee its construction.

It didn't bother Johnson that people assumed Scotty was building a mansion for himself with profits from his gold. Scotty was happy to perpetuate the idea. Johnson seemed amused with the stories and never told them anything different.

Joe and Scotty spent time together doing some heavy drinking followed by sleeping in the horse barn near the building that became known as Scotty's Castle. Both of these men were risk-takers and not afraid of consequences. A sense of kinship developed and was part of their friendship. Years later, during times of financial need, it was Frank E. Scott, a relative of Scotty, who remembered that kinship and, it seems, became a patron to Joe.

Today, Scotty's Castle is one of the most famous of Death Valley tourist attractions.

8

THE HILLS, THE MOUNTAINS, AND THE DESERT

Success, the mark no mortal wit, or surest hand can always hit, for whatsoe'er we perpetrate, we do but row we're steer'd by fate.

—Samuel Butler

During the few years when I was able to make annual visits, it was my pleasure to have Joe act as tour guide and show me many of the wonders that he had discovered. He had a love for the beauty and vastness of the Nevadan and Californian mountains and deserts.

There were many paths off the main roads where I saw such surprises as Ubehebe Crater, Devil's Golf Course, Mosaic Canyon, Devil's Hole, and my favorite, the Cathedral in the Desert. This country was much more than a colorless, dried up, and uninhabitable land. Alongside stark landscapes was a world of majestic beauty and wonders seldom seen elsewhere.

As we drove along valley roads, Joe would point to hollows that could be seen high up on the sides of scarred mountains. He said that the holes had been dug over the years by other prospectors.

When I asked him how men could get to those places without paths or roads, he replied that they did what he did. They climbed the mountains carrying shovels, picks, and ropes. Gazing at the distant ridges and peaks, Joe tried to give me a mini crash course of their geological history and composition; the volcanic action from which they had sprung; the resulting faults, and the presence of cracked shifting rocks. He explained that his diggings had often been successful, and it was at these times when the real work began.

Among Joe's many producing mines were talc, dolomite, silver, and wollastonite. He had collections of ore samples and the equipment to assay the samples. *As a gift, he packaged and labeled about twenty-five different kinds and gave them to me.*

Joe explained that in order to be able to work some of the mines, he often had to build and maintain his own roads, invest in heavy equipment, and hire crews. There were a few photos taken at some of the locations that clearly showed what this looked like.

One such mine was called Jacob's Wonder. It was located in the Panamint Mountain Range near the ghost town of Panamint City. The city had been deserted when Joe discovered silver ore. He laid his claim to the entire area, obtaining title to Panamint City and its *castle.*

In order to be able to work this mine, Joe needed to rebuild multiple sections along nine miles of road up to the elevation of 8,500 feet. This allowed him to bring in his heavy equipment to build a complete silver-extraction plant. The climb was steep. The work was hot, dusty, and exhausting. Living conditions were primitive at best. However difficult it was, the gratification was in the success of delivering a satisfactory grade of silver ore. With the help of hired hands, the silver was extracted and made into dore (unrefined bars). Considering that the ore was better than money in the bank, he stashed away more than a few bars and kept them locked in a storage trailer.

Today, Panamint City is once again a *ghost town.* Joe experienced a not uncommon set of reversals. He was forced out of Jacob's Wonder by frequent wash-outs along the road, the poor price of silver, and the encroachment of the National Park System. A good deal of equipment had to be abandoned, but he would not abandon his passion for mining. No matter how long the search; no matter how tough the circumstances; no matter how many failures; there was a thrill of discovery that blocked out all the frustrations and disappointments.

Because mining was such an expensive proposition, Joe had to find ways to finance his own expeditions. Income came from a variety of irregular and creative sources and provided stakes when they were needed.

Joe, the risk-taker, was proud of some of his accomplishments in that area. He recalled, with relish, that he had pocketed high profits by contracting with the military to retrieve spent shells from a gunnery range.

From 1942 *to* 1945, *the Mojave Desert was being used as an army training field by General George Pat-*

ten. Before the end of WWII, almost every corner had been occupied by troops being rotated in and out. Records show that 190,000 *soldiers eventually trained there using* 38,000 *military armored vehicles. The Chocolate Mountains area was used as a gunnery range. By* 1947, *this land was being cleared of minefields and gun shells.*

In a faintly related field, Joe built and operated a tungsten recovery plant in the 1950s. The material was used for armor-plated weapons during the Korean War. Although profitable, this was a short-lived business. It seems that the government opened a tungsten mine in Korea that broke the market and shut down his plant.

Another opportunity for Joe to produce an income arose with the California building boom. Homeowners were glad to hire him to do stonework for them. He had found some land that had excellent, colorful stone for fireplaces, siding, and stone fences. It was his favorite and his most popular building material.

His dabbling in mineralogy may have helped him to locate the stones, but he found out, too late, that the stones contained uranium. *Navajo Indians in Arizona knew where deposits of uraninite were located and there is also the possibility that they may have introduced*

Joe to this ore from which uranium is obtained. Uranium itself is a silvery gray, metallic-looking mineral that corrodes to a spaling black oxide coat in the air.

Joe probably would have obtained the uraninite from an open pit, using drilling and blasting, before excavation with a loader and dump truck. He wouldn't have expected that there was danger from airborne dust exposure or such a thing as radon gas. Joe remembered that the education was costly because he found himself in major trouble with the authorities and was ordered to go back and remove all the stones that he had labored so long and so hard to mine and then set.

Working in this type of business prepared him for another project. Joe was needed back home.

There had been a fire that had badly damaged Joe's parent's home, and he was asked, by his brothers, to help rebuild on another site on the property. It was payback time for all the grief that he had put them through in the past. Although his heart was always in the West, he answered the call and drove cross-country to help.

It was summer and the work went quickly. It wasn't long before the family was able to move into the new small two-story cottage.

The house was built on high ground and wasn't complete until it was covered with large, colorful stone that came from a riverbed in the valley below.

There was no danger that the stones contained uranium this time. Joe had become quite an accomplished stone mason, and his brothers were satisfied.

9

THE PROSPECTOR AND THE BUSINESSMAN

Every calling is great when greatly pursued.

—Oliver Wendell Holmes, Jr.

The history of each of the mining claims that Joe recorded lies in the files of Bureau of Land Management (BLM) and U.S Department of the Interior. Once he started exploring, he was hooked on prospecting.

Joe conducted business with the same renegade attitude that took him to the Yucatan. He claimed the title of *geologist* for himself. His voracious appetite for learning and the years spent living on the land and working it seemed to indicate that the title was earned. Mining claims that showed high promise were sold in Canada and were cash transactions that left no records. There were few witnesses to these deals; however, two of Joe's brothers were present in a Las Vegas motel where they met with him to celebrate one such sale. They never forgot the suitcase that he dumped on the table that had contained undeclared income of, what appeared to be, $1 million in bills.

In the United States, there is an ongoing debate as to whether the federal government has the Constitutional right to place an income tax on its citizens. Joe held firmly to the belief that the income tax violated his civil rights and took a special satisfaction in evading the tax. He did, however, accept the fact that fees associated with mining were a necessary and valid part of doing business, though the fight was on when authorities decided they could increase the fees with the goal of driving miners off of their properties.

> The income tax has made more liars out of American people than golf has.
>
> —Will Rogers

Proof that some of Joe's mining paid off shows up in the many business ventures that he had invested in. But it appears that even though he had put his money into his businesses, he hadn't really put his heart into them. He was happiest with his pick and shovel. We can but speculate why this was.

Probably more than any other motivators, what really drove Joe on, were the elements of danger, facing extremes, setting records, and living to tell about it. He possessed some of the same metal as Captain John Fremont and Bridger, our early pioneers and pathfinders. As he traversed the West alone, he would park his truck and go packing into danger zones with what he could carry on his back.

By the end of the 1930s, Joe had enough money to invest in a business venture in Baker, a small desert town in California. He bought a burned-out café and twenty cabins on a forty-acre lot that straddled Highway 91, now *Baker Boulevard.* Over the next few years, he rebuilt the café and added a lounge and a gas station.

Baker was an ideal jumping-off-point from which Joe could search for and reach mineral riches. It was also a good business location. There was a steady flow of Californians traveling the well paved highway that wove directly through the town. Customers were often the high-spirited, partying Hollywood crowd looking for excitement and making their way to the thriving Las Vegas casinos that were ninety miles from Baker.

This was still the era when there were few good roads and getting stranded could be dangerous. It is not uncommon for the temperatures, in Baker, to reach 113 degrees. Not more than a stone's throw away is the entrance to Death Valley, where temperatures have been know to reach 135° F. Travelers drove in cars with their windows open to try to stay cool as they sped along the road between the Death Valley Desert to the north and the Mojave Desert to the south. By the time they would arrive in Baker, they would certainly have been parched and looking for something cool to drink, some water for their radiators, and some gas to fill their tanks.

As described many years later in the *Baker Valley News,* September 16, 1994 issue, one of Joe's buildings eventually became one of the most attractive buildings in Baker. "He faced the structure with flagstone from a quarry near Stateline. That, combined with large plate glass windows and an upward angled canopy gave the building a very distinctive appearance. The hardware store, Laundromat, Wells Fargo Motel, site of the new KOA and (across the street) the X-Cel station and the site of the new Baker Del Taco, occupy the land now."

Sometime in the early part of WWII, Joe's plans were interrupted. It is known that Joe was drafted into the army and stationed in Texas. Conforming to this structured environment was so stressful and alien to his nature that it appeared he wasn't a very good soldier. He developed stomach ulcers and was granted a medical discharge and returned to Baker. It is believed that it wasn't long before he was again prospecting

It should be no surprise that each fortune that Joe made ended up being put back into the ground as he added to his collection of leases on mines for the rest of his life. He was a speculator, and a speculator he would always be.

During this time, Johnnie, one of Joe's brothers, was in the infantry and saw action in Sicily, as well as action during the deadly invasion on Omaha Beach. Another brother, Frank, saw enemy action in the Coast Guard. While in the service, his ship was attacked and sunk. Six years later during the Korean War, in what was described as a "Police Action," two more brothers enlisted in the army.

10

MARRIAGE AND THE MINER

> It is well for a man to respect his own vocation whatever it is and to think himself bound to uphold it and to claim for it the respect it deserves.
>
> —Charles Dickens (1812–1870)

It was in the late 1940s and into the 1950s that Joe tried to lead a little more settled life. In the course of his travels, he had stopped in New York. There he met Rae, a petite, pretty, dark-haired, and enchanting ballerina. He was smitten and pursued her relentlessly, determined to have her as his wife.

Joe was unique in that he had the abilities of a chameleon. He could change his image from that of rattle-trap-truck-driving-desert rat to a "sports-car-driving playboy to a black-tie-Wall-Street banker.

This chameleon could be gentlemanly and well spoken, especially when among women. He must have been a convincing salesman because Rae accepted his proposal.

It was while in Baker that he married, and it was there that he brought his new bride to live. Next to his stint in the army, adapting to a settled lifestyle may have been the most difficult thing that Joe had ever attempted to do.

Their life together was a tumultuous one. She was a genteel, city-bred, naïve, young woman living in a secure setting and raising her young son. She had no idea that she would be leaving that security behind forever, and many times during their marriage, she expressed deep regret at the circumstances that she found herself in. Although Joe could be warm-hearted and generous, the wanderlust never left him.

While still living in Baker, Rae gave birth to a daughter. As their circumstances changed, there were times during their marriage when they lived in luxury and times of poverty.

The whole West was Joe's playground. That inevitably led to the idea of making frequent pilgrimages into Mexico. The landscape, the people, and the music of the country held an attraction for him that his wife shared. There were pleasure trips and shopping trips. But, for many years, there also were annual trips to an orphanage.

> I expect to pass through life but once. If therefore, there be any kindness I can show, or any good thing I can do to any fellow being, let me do it now, and not defer or neglect it, as I shall not pass this way again.
>
> —William Penn (1644–1718)

On their first trips to Mexico, Joe and Rae could not help but see the abject squalor that was the sprawling blight across the face of the country. They would see shelters that most often consisted of bits and pieces of metal, wood, and cardboard and note that the more fortunate were living in small one room hovels that had no doors or windows.

During shopping trips, Joe and Rae would be approached by children, of all ages, who lived in the cities and towns. These were kids who would put down pieces of cardboard, on which they would sleep at night. If they slept in front of the shops of the local merchants they knew that they would be awake as soon as the first shoppers arrived. Tourists would be the best targets for handouts. If the little street urchins stayed well enough, they were able to survive on the few coins that they collected.

Acres of trash inevitably accumulated at the very edges of every town. On the drive in and again on the drive out, Joe and Rae could see the scores of small children as they scavenged up and down the mounds of garbage, for anything useable. This made them sad and they were deeply touched.

Joe understood the certain truth that, in his world, opportunity lay just around every corner; but that was not true, in Mexico, for these children. It made him want to do more than put quarters into the palms of a few of the children. The realistic conclusion that he came to was that, if there was a chance for the children to have a future, they not only needed food, clothing, and shelter, they also needed to be loved and educated.

It was a small step from there for Joe to decide that he should be supporting those who were taking the children in. After a little searching, he was able to find Mexican orphanages where only the most destitute; the deserted foundlings; and the sick and orphaned children were brought. Many of the orphanages were so barren that 90 people would be obliged to share one outhouse. Orphanages were often run, under the most primitive conditions, by devoted, hard working, caring people. The list of needs was inexhaustible.

Joe and Rae would no longer be satisfied to ignore the poverty-stricken children. They would no longer ignore the vision of children scavenging for food and they accepted the challenge to bring help and comfort to them. This was the beginning of their well planned annual pilgrimages. The trips were made with a pickup truck that they would spend weeks loading with food and clothing. Last to be loaded were the cases of hot dogs that they knew would be eaten with huge grins on hungry faces.

Few people were ever told about these special visits. It was just their delight to be greeted with shrieks of delight as expectant children would come running, through the dusty yard, and cling to them with hugs. Joe and Rae spoke of how little it took to make the children of the orphanage happy.

During this shared experience between husband and wife, their finest qualities blossomed. There was pure joy in their faces as they talked about loving and caring and spending themselves to bring some small comforts to these rescued, barefoot, cherub-like little people. It was a satisfaction to know that, by their small gifts, they were contributing to new hope for a brighter future for the children.

11

WHERE 'ERE THE WIND BLOWS

> Courage is a quality so necessary for maintaining virtue that it is always respected, even when it is associated with vice.
>
> —Samuel Johnson (1709–1784)

Back in 1945, WWII was over and Joe's two brothers had been discharged from the military. The country was inundated by returning servicemen and found itself with several new dilemmas.

The war had been had been fought by courageous, but often, very young men. They wholeheartedly wanted to pick up their lives again, but it soon became clear that getting jobs and adequate housing would be major challenges. Now that the need for weapons production no longer existed, manufacturers were speedily trying to re-tool their factories to produce peacetime products.

In order to provide the adequate housing, American ingenuity kicked in and prefab housing was born. Wingfoot homes, about the size of a small trailer home, were mass-produced and sent to all corners of the land. But while these things were taking place, Joe's brothers were at loose ends.

Joe, again, successfully used his salesmanship ability to convince his brothers to come to Baker and help him run the business. For a short period, a third brother joined them.

Just like Joe's wife, Rae, they all came to regret their decisions. This was hot, dry, desert land, and the work was tedious as well as monotonous for these young folks. The pay was not always there, and at best, it was poor.

It didn't take long to notice that once Joe was relieved of the responsibilities of running the business, he was off prospecting again. He could be gone for days or weeks and sometimes only returned to take money out of the till to fund more prospecting. They soon discovered that even this could get worse.

In his eagerness to develop his claims, Joe began to accumulate debts that he could not pay back in a timely fashion. He seemed to be obsessed with the miner's life.

When the bills began to arrive with Joe's name on them, creditors began to look to the brothers to settle the debts. It doesn't take much imagination to picture the kind of reactions that appeared on their faces. Undoubtedly, they would have made use of a very large, well developed, colorful vocabulary of four letter words that they had picked up before the end of their military service. The personal impact became so negative that they felt forced into changing their surnames in order to protect themselves.

When Joe found out about the name changes, he was unflustered and decided that this was such a brilliant idea that he changed his name also. Thus, the names of these brothers were permanently changed from Ostrenga to Ostrenger.

This seemed perfectly logical to Joe. It does appear, though, that over the years, he was prone to change the spelling of his surname by whim. His signature often appears with the middle e changed to an i. He could rationalize that since the family name in

Poland had been Ostre'ga, another name change was only natural. However, his brothers did not take to the name change as well. It always remained a sore spot for them and they left Baker as soon as they could. Without his brothers, Joe needed a partner to help his wife run the business. Sixty years later, the brothers had all greatly mellowed, and yet, the very mention of those days, in Baker, could still trigger a noticeable bristling chill.

The Baker property was eventually sold to a Realty company when Joe's partner in the café sold his interests to a businessman by the name of Ted Reetz. In addition to the $400,000 cash Joe received for the sale of his property, he was given some *worthless* lakefront property on Lake Arrowhead that the Realty company wanted to get rid of.

Joe considered the land was a nuisance and dumped it in a quick turnover, cash deal. Relieved of that business, he was free to prospect full time.

The smell of danger was in Joe's nostrils. Challenging the elements and winning, was the unrelenting driving force that drew him back to the nomadic life time and again. It even overshadowed the excitement of the discovery of mineral rich ore.

Joe exposed himself to the dangers of deserts and mountains; areas of barren desolation; landscapes void of human habitation; temperatures that burned up body moisture as fast as it could be replaced; and mountain storms and slides that were deadly traps.

In order to accomplish these feats, Joe had the good sense to prepare himself. It didn't always come from reading journals. As Army Rangers are trained in survival skills, so it was that he took great pains to train.

Wherever he would go, Joe would take the time to talk to everyone he met. This talk was not for idle purposes. He used every opportunity to learn from Native Americans of such nations as the Timbisha Shoshone and the Navajo. This was their territory and they had a knowledge of trails, paths, water holes, and minerals. He met other miners and geologists. More than once, their talk was over a good bottle of whiskey. But, he learned from them. He said, "I know where the water is. I've been in these parts long enough to be able to live without help."

Throughout his travels, as he was able to overcome the worst obstacles that nature could throw at him, there was an undeniable sense of the joy of victory. He survived!

Years later, in the telling of the story, Joe had to laugh about the Lake Arrowhead nuisance that he had sold. He never forgot the joke was on him as the land values skyrocketed.

12

THE MOTHER LODE AND DISASTER

Success covers a multitude of blunders.

—George Bernard Shaw

There occurred an interlude of normalcy during which Joe pulled himself away from his diggings long enough to bring his family from the desert to the Pacific and to a real home. It actually gave him a chance to catch up on current events and take an active role in the activities of the miners' union and political movements.

It was a happy day for Joe's family when they moved to the new, modern, upscale home that he had built for them in the hills of San Fernando, California.

The family lifestyle was comfortable and interesting. The kids were growing up and found new friends. Their home was close enough to Hollywood for them to rub shoulders with up-and-coming stars and starlets.

Joe's wanderings did not cease, and his adventures continued. However, except for his excursions into wilderness areas, the family's lives were not much different than those of their neighbors.

They remained in their San Fernando residence in surroundings that were much better suited to Joe's little, city-born wife. The opportunities for a social life, for entertainment, and for shopping were just around the corner in Beverly Hills and in Los Angeles. Settling in the community had been a good decision for the family, and they thrived.

San Fernando was also a pleasant place for business operations. It was here that modern conveniences were brought to bear. There were papers to file and fees to pay for every new mining lease. Buyers were needed for the most promising mines. There were contacts to make, properties to sell, and contracts to seal. As an owner and operator of working mines, he needed to hire competent help, obtain and transport the machinery, and supervise the work.

The children reached adulthood and their independence.

Although Rae had been happy and felt protected in that home, a day came when she had suffered a severe fright that caused her to want to leave. The trigger of this fright began with an early morning earthquake.

Their house had been built on one of the beautiful California hills. The real danger was not from the earthquake, itself, but rather from the collapse of the water tower that was located higher on the hill and above their house. The water released from the toppled tower rushed down the hill creating mudslides that buried the houses below.

The family narrowly escaped as they ran from their house in their nightclothes. Though the house was restored, it was sold. Rae contented herself with apartment living.

> It is a blessed thing that in every age some one has had the individuality enough and courage enough to stand by his own convictions.
>
> —Robert G. Ingersoll (1933–1800)

> My riches consist not in the extent of my possessions, but in the fewness of my wants.
>
> —J.Brotherton

During the time when Hunter Mountain and Death Valley were open to prospecting, Joe was looking for gold again. He didn't find much gold, but he recognized a massive deposit of wollastonite. This is a valuable nonmetallic mineral used, among many other things, as a substitute for asbestos and used to save fuel in firing ceramics.

Joe estimated that the vein of wollasonite was 105 feet deep and four and one-half miles long. This was more than enough for the mining world to take notice. According to the California State Division of Mines and Geology, the U.S. Bureau of Mines, and the Geological Survey of Great Britain, Joe's deposit was the largest known deposit in the world.

Joe believed that the ore that he had assayed was 99-percent pure and priceless. His appetite had been whetted by multiple smaller, very promising, discoveries of other minerals over the years. But now, it seemed that he had found and laid claim to the "mother lode."

He knew that this alone did not insure instant riches. There was still a long way to go.

Even though his claims were eating away more of his cash reserves, it was the cost of doing business and he loved the rugged life. He didn't worry about comforts. But, this was not the case for his wife.

Any assets that had ever been acquired had been converted to cash to support Joe's appetite for mining. Rae had to suffer through a nomadic life, often spending days living alone in a camper in the hot desert.

Going by past experience, Joe had confidence that he could close some good deals on his new claims. But, as the months went by, the deals did not always keep up with his operating expenses. It must be remembered that he had one of the most valuable properties in the West. Developing the wollastonite mine would be a daunting task for any mega corporation, but up to this point, his was a one-man operation. This operation would be years in the making.

Desert living took the greatest toll on Joe's wife, Rae. This couple's wealth was still stuck in the ground when the Desert Closure Act came along. In one sweep, miners' rights that had been guaranteed by the GML (General Mining Law) were ripped away. The scales of justice became unbalanced as miners lost their ability to earn a living in their profession. Rae's final home was a trailer house in Pahrump, Nevada. It was during this period, and after many years of wandering together, that Rae came to the end of her life.

13

A TIME TO FIGHT

An act of the legislature, repugnant to the constitution, is void.

—John Marshall (1755–1835)

(When a corrupt official hasn't a leg to stand on, he stands on his constitutional rights)

As reported in the *Baker Valley News* on September 16, 1994, Joe had claims on approximately twenty square miles of bentonite, manganese, and wolastonite in Saline Valley near the Death Valley National Monument. He was paying filing and recording fees plus annual lease fees on 125 key claims and numerous other prospects in Inyo County outside of Death Valley National Monument.

Joe knew his rights and understood that the General Mining Law (GML) permitted persons to prospect and make claim where they found mineral deposits on public lands that were not otherwise declared closed by the GML. The cost per claim for the right to develop the ore was $100 paid to the federal government annually. Full title (a patent) to the property cost a miner $2.50 an acre (i.e. twenty acres was $50). Joe had claims on approximately twenty square miles. However, the real cost according to the Nevada Bureau of Land Management was nearly $40,000 per claim just for the *right to mine.* The development costs would then begin (multiply by 125 key claims).

Joe was well aware that the Desert Closure Act was the successful result of efforts by the Environmental Protection Agency and special interest groups. The act affected that right to mine and banned miners, in many cases, from even putting foot on their claims.

COMMENTARY:

The incredible story of the growth of special interest groups and their influence on the nation's political systems has the appearance of global intrigue and is a convoluted study. It raises such questions as: *How could the state of Nevada have been forced to give up control of more than 88 percent of its territory to the federal government, despite the public outcry by its citizens and its elected officials? What is the true purpose of land takeovers? What agencies are involved? (Eleven western states have been the objects of this kind of takeover.)

It should be noted that the Secretary of the Interior is one of the most important figures in the West and runs what has become one of the largest of Washington bureaucracies. He has charge of the National Park Service, the Bureau of Land Management, the Fish and Wildlife Service, the Bureau of Reclamation, the Bureau of Indian Affairs, the Geological Survey, and the Bureau of Mines.

Other land is under the control of the Department of Agriculture, which has charge of the U.S. Forest Service. Smaller land holdings belong to the branches of the military.

Each of the controlling entities has its own statutory basis and its own laws, which are totally different from one another. They have different objectives and obligations that require self-perpetual motion machines called bureaucracies.

There was a time when these agencies most often served the public interest. Now, national and international environmental groups, as well as thousands of individual environmentalists, are holding sway. Stalling tactics and court appeals have proven successful for their causes. These groups have their own agendas. It should not be confused with the public good as understood by the framers of the U.S. Constitution or as understood by the general public.

Even those programs with worthy causes are often managed or mismanaged by staffers who were never elected to any kind of official post. When it happens that they take the law and interpret it to suit their own ideas, they are circumventing the law. Such practices have created virtual czars. Enough czars can control the nation's economy.

Officials using such tactics suffer a loss of respect and loss of honor while the American public suffers the loss of more of their constitutional rights.

EXAMPLES:

Loss of State's Rights: Growing for the worthy causes of equality of education, or protection of endangered species, or wilderness protection.

Swelling Executive Powers: Growing for the purpose of *enhancing minority rights*, or for getting through an *energy crisis*, or for *the sake of peace*. Unbridled misuse of power in government agencies has become so common that special efforts must be made to explain government actions that have led to the coining of the phrase "putting a spin on the news."

Based on these observations, the question arises that asks what is happening in the courts where citizens are losing their appeals for their state's rights and for their property rights?

Citizens who wish to be informed must undertake a search for the answers. The answers are not easily found in this country's media, which we so proudly call the "free press." Too many newspapers, magazines, and TV broadcasting companies are owned by and receive their direction from special interest groups and have lost their objectivity.

Examples on the exercise of power exerted on reporters: *Chase Manhattan Bank owns stock in ABC, CBS, and NBC. *More pressure is applied by the newswriters' own guild that promotes their union's liberal agenda.

The CFR (Council of Foreign Relations) has its own goals. *Among the members of the CFR:* ABC: Peter Jennings, David Brinkley, John Scali, Barbara Walters; CBS: Wm Paley, Dan Rather, Harry Reasoner, and Bill Moyer; NBC: Tom Brokow, John Chancellor, Marvin Kalb, Irving R. Levine; CNN: Daniel Shorr; PBS: Robert McNeil, John Lehrer

The Desert Closure Act, S-21, expanded Death Valley National Monument from 2.2 million acres to 3.5 million acres and designated more of it a National Park and Desert Wilderness Area. The act closed all these areas to mineral entry and closed about 25,000 miles of back country to public use.

Following the Desert Closure Act, Joe's claims and personal property, including mining equipment, were off limits.

Joe had tied up most of his assets in his claims, and there was no way to recover these investments. Yet, he realized that if he did not continue to pay the fees on the claims, forfeiture would be automatic. Part of his fight took place when the fees he tried to pay were refused. It took face-to-face confrontations and a bold stance on Joe's part for the fees to be accepted.

He had no qualms about shaking his fist at ranking politicians on courthouse steps.

By now, Joe was adamant that he would not give in to the government landgrab without a fight. Claiming his rights under the GML, Joe first began to take legal action in 1989. He filed two lawsuits against the Bureau of Land Management, Attorney General Janet Reno, Secretary of Interior Bruce Babbitt (personally), and the Department of the Interior.

His fight was followed in local newspapers, but Joe gained some national public notoriety when an interview that he gave to a CBN reporter on the 700 Club was televised. The interview was part of a documentary called *War on the West.*

The miners' unions of California, Arizona, and Nevada were aggressively using all legal means at their disposal also. Joe was seen carrying protest signs, alongside other miners, during union rallies and during confrontations and obstructionist activities.

In addition to the 700 Club documentary, there were interviews and photographs by newspaper reporters that recorded Joe's activities. According to Joe, as told to Donald Fife and also to this writer, "Only one in five thousand mining claims produces a paying mine. I guess I beat the odds. It has taken me forty years of my life and my life savings to develop and prove this deposit. Now Feinstein and the Sierra Club have me in a National Park and United Nations World Biosphere Zone. As Secretary of the Interior Hodel told the Osage Indians when the environmentalists wanted to make a Prairieland Park out of their oil lands in Oklahoma a few years ago, 'As night follows day, the National Park Service will kick you out sooner rather than later.'"

One of our visits included a drive to Baker, California. Joe took us to the site of his former businesses and reminisced. He introduced himself to a gentleman who was interested in finding out why we were there. As Joe suspected, this was a fellow miner. When the miner was asked how he and other miners were doing, he answered that they were pretty effectively shut down and were giving up. Those of us in the Midwest rarely heard anything about the miners' fights. If the news found its way to the national media, it was buried or played down.

14

DOWN BUT NOT OUT

To be vanquished and yet not surrender, that is victory.

—Josef Pilsudski

In 1994, Joe was still waiting for the courts to take action on his lawsuits when he decided it was time for a change. If the government was determined to handcuff mining in the U.S., he would take his prospecting somewhere else.

Joe said, "I know the heat belt from the North Pole to the Equator and the volcanic activity that makes the minerals. I know where to look for gold. I walk on the ground and make a mental note of it, analyzing it. I do my own testing, assaying, and lab work. If the formation is promising, I test the ground and just keep on checking."

Without going into great detail, Joe went on to say, "I went to Costa Rica. In less than thirty days, I found gold. I contacted the Costa Rican officials and presented my qualifications and credentials. The government owns the ground. But there is a man with an old Spanish land grant who said he owns the land and he had to be dealt with."

As Joe's story goes, after meeting with officials in the presidential residence, a deal was worked out with Joe, whereby the Costa Rican government and the holder of the Spanish land grant would permit mining. They would receive 5 percent of the profits.

After expenses, the profits were then to be split between Joe and a partner who had agreed to bankroll the whole operation. The plan was, "I'll just set up the operation and let hired men, who I know are trustworthy, run it. In two years, the operation should be ready to go. I built metal recovery plants in less time than it takes an architect to draw the plans."

At the age of eighty-four, Joe still had the spirit of the speculator. His mind continued to contrive plans as though he were indestructible. He had a will that did not want to accept defeat despite seemingly impenetrable barriers.

The whole story about Joe's excursions into Costa Rica and what the possible outcome would have been to the business deals he was working on are now left up to the imagination. His time was running out.

Costa Rica is a relatively wealthy, respectable democracy. Starting in the 1990s, *grassroots explorers have been active in locating multiple gold fields in the Central American countries. The epithermal geological explanation for the creation of gold deposits can be found on the web. Mining production had a surge after the price of gold soared in* 2003. *Government royalties from the mining companies are in the* 2-*percent range.*

15

MAKING THE BEST OF IT

I've read the last page of the Bible.
It's going to turn out all right.

—Billy Graham

By the time I last saw Joe in 1997, he had been diagnosed with bladder cancer. His strength was ebbing. He had not returned to Costa Rica to carry out his plans. His resources had been depleted, and he was living on a little social security check. There was still a lot of determination left in him, but a little less fight. His lawsuits were still pending, and he wasn't going to drop them. Circumstances had changed, and he had made a choice to sell his interests in the wollastonite mine for a fraction of it's worth.

I waited for him outside a bank building during a meeting that he told me was with Las Vegas businessman, Frank E. Scott. After the meeting, he handed me a signed and dated copy of a contract for the conditional sale of the wollastonite mine to Ely J. Ades and Frank E. Scott. The agreed upon sale price was $3,000,000. The condition of the sale was that "the claims would be clear of any liens, encumbrances, royalty payments, and any other." The date on the agreement was January 21, 1997. Upon signing the agreement, he was given a check of $3,000 earnest money.

This simple contract was a sign that Joe had come to the realization that he would never live to develop the prize of his lifetime nor would he live to see the profits that his wollastonite mine could one day produce. His satisfaction was in knowing that he had gained recognition for a "world-class" discovery. It was in that knowledge that he took the steps needed to tie up his financial affairs. With that done, he settled into a wait-and-see mode.

Joe's lawsuits, that would affect his estate, were still on the court's agenda and were being followed by interested parties on both sides of the issue. He had received a certain amount of satisfaction from the attention that the GML dispute had raised and it pays to note from which quarter his notoriety was coming.

There was an excitement in the mining world as the wollastonite discovery had been gaining the attention of mining journals and had become big news in local newspapers. Credit needs to be given to one of Joe's biggest and most renowned supporters in the world of professional geologists.

It was Don Fife, Former Reagan-Bush Appointee/Advisor for Geology, Energy and Minerals for the California Desert Advisory Board (1981–1989) who recognized the tremendous potential of Joe's wollastonite deposit, but who also recognized the multiple political powers and unlimited resources of environmentalists and special interests groups that were behind the battle that Joe was involved in. It was Don Fife who stayed in touch with Joe and reported on the struggle over the wollastonite mine as it evolved. He has generously shared some stories that Joe told him over the years.

As reported by Don Fife, "During the 1990s, when Senators Boxer and Feinstein were turning the California Desert into a United Nations World Man in the

Biosphere preserve, Joe along with thousands of small miners and ranchers had their property rights stolen by the environmentalists and their lackeys in Congress. Joe had found and staked the world's largest wollastonite deposit on Hunter Mountain on the south west margin of Death Valley in Inyo County, California.

When Joe went to the Death Valley office to file his assessment work or proof of annual labor, he was surprised that all the *bureaucrats* at the Office were treating him with respect for the first time. For a change, they didn't hassle him when he was filing his mining claims' "annual assessment work or intent to hold" for claims that somehow "migrated" to the inside of the National Monument boundaries!

Joe gave them a piece of his mind, as usual, but surprisingly, he got no static back. He used to say, "The bureaucrats treat me like Rodney Dangerfield. They don't give us miners any respect." But, as he was leaving the Death Valley Monument headquarters, on this particular day, all the staffers, pulled out recent articles crediting Joe with discovering the world's largest wollastonite deposit. They asked Joe to autograph the articles published in magazines and newspapers, many of which had been written by myself.

Joe was so overwhelmed that he tried to call me after leaving Death Valley. I had locked myself in my office to compose some twenty pages of testimony for a congressional hearing on the mining law. I did not answer the phone all day. When he could get me on the phone, he told me what had happened and drove the 200 miles to my office in Tustin. I heard a knock on my door and there was Joe! He was the happiest man I ever saw. We went to a nearby Denny's where Joe bought my coffee. As tears streamed down his face, he said, "Don, you have made me famous. I never dreamed that anyone would want me to autograph anything!" I made Joe pose for a couple of photos. One was used for an article on the J.O. Wollastonite Mine.

Joe Ostrenger was the real thing right out of the wild west.

He used to tell of how he worked with the owner of the Slulfide Queen Silver/lead Mine, at Mountain Pass between Baker and the Nevada State Line. Prim Resort and Casino is there today.

It was in the 1920s and or the 1930s when they crushed and milled the silver ore into a concentrate that was sent off to a smelter or refinery in Salt Lake City or San Francisco. These refineries had numerous fees or penalties if the raw silver concentrate didn't meet certain standards, plus the cost of transportation. This was before the Uranium rush of the 1940s and 1950s that lead to the discovery of one of the world's largest rare earth deposits, now operated by Cheron Minerals.

Joe said they built a refinery to purify silver from the metal concentrates. The refined silver was very pure. Joe and the owner decided they would see if they could mint some silver dollars. Wow, they looked just like the real McCoy. They took a batch into Las Vegas where they spent them just like the ones made at U.S. Mints. Why send the ore concentrates to the smelters in Salt Lake City or San Francisco, when you could cut out all cost of refining and transportation? The Slulfide Queen Silver Dollars were actually pure silver. Real silver dollars had a small percentage of alloy to harden them so they would wear better and longer. According to Joe, nobody was being cheated as there was actually more silver content than those minted by the government.

Another story Joe used to tell happened when he was struggling to build his business (motel & gas station) in Baker. A couple of San Bernardino building inspectors turned up without warning. They started criticizing Joe's work. Joe put up with their criticism for a while. After a few hints, Joe got the impression they wanted a bribe. So he told them he would have to go inside to get his wallet. But Joe came out waving a loaded pistol! "Get off my land or I will fill you full of lead! Get out of town or you will have to be carried out and don't ever come back to Baker if you know what's good for you." It is rumored that Baker never saw a San Bernardino County building inspector till after the Korean War twenty years later!

The present condition of Death Valley bears no resemblance to the Death Valley Days television series that was hosted by Ronald Reagan for many years. Death Valley National Park hosts a fall 49ers' Jamboree or campout honoring and venerating the prospectors of the old west; Death Valley Scotty, One-Eyed Thompson, Seldom Seen Slim, Shorty Harris, etc. However when these organizers meet the real live prospector, in the form of Joe Ostrenger, who has performed a national service by finding the world's largest wollastonite deposit, they treat him like dirt. They can't wait to violate his civil and property rights and to run him out of their "empire" which they have turned into a United Nations World Heritage Site without a vote of Congress or the citizens of the United States."

16

THE STORIES END

It's a wise man who lives with money in the bank;
It's a fool who dies that way.

French Proverb

Though he was experiencing the physical discomforts of his bladder cancer, Joe made the decision to treat himself. It seems that his distrust of medical practices was cemented in the memory of significant flash burn injuries that his wife had gotten during a surgical procedure. Since that incident, he carried too much anger to put himself in the hands of the health care system.

Self-diagnosis and self-treatment were not new ideas to Joe. He didn't consider surgery an option and had been taking care of an abdominal hernia on his own for years. A leather hernia belt seemed to satisfy his needs and could easily be seen as he buckled it over the top of his trousers.

That Joe would decide to treat his own cancer without medical intervention was no surprise. He believed that his own pharmacology was a match for anything that a physician would prescribe. His choice of medication was a tincture of silver. Drawing from the supply of silver that he had already mined, he played the role of pharmacist and prepared his own prescription Other medication was over the counter and purchased in Mexico.

The wheels of justice move slowly—sometimes in the wrong direction and sometimes not at all. However, it appears that in 1998 the Ninth District Court finally reached a decision on the wollestonite mine in Joe's favor.

Unfortunately, despite his best efforts, he was by now no longer able to care for himself and needed nursing care. News of the court's decision reached Joe in a Las Vegas hospital. It is hoped that there was satisfaction in the hearing of this news. He would no longer be concerned with the final disposition of his properties.

Joe's life had been extravagantly spent blazing trails and enjoying the thrill of discovery. His life exemplified the struggle between the two natures that we all possess. That the good and honorable side achieved dominance became evident in his last days. His hospitalization provided the backdrop for mending relationships. There was comfort in the coming together with his daughter and her children. There was time to talk and reconcile with his brothers. There was time to pray and to renew his Christian faith. Then, he left again, on this, his last journey.

The man, Joe, lived a great part of his life in the solitude of the wilderness and in isolation from the world, as we know it. We'll never know the experiences that he enjoyed or suffered through, except for the few that he shared. Those of us who knew him have had the privilege to grasp glimpses of the spirit that drove him on.

The wollastonite mine was deeply buried with financial and environmental encumbrances. As of this writing, it remains untouchable, with no foreseeable chance of being opened anytime soon.

Haying on the Ostrenga farm in WI

Joe visiting his birthplace in Birch Creek, MI

Walter and Joe in Pahrump, NV

Joe's mother, with Margaret and Norman in Las Vegas Casino

Nieces, Peg and Jane with Joe and the Malachite table

Walter with Joe outside work shed in Pahrump, NV

Joe, Margaret, and Walter at Scotty's Castle in Grapevine Canyon

Two hired hands with Joe at the Panamint City Silver Mine

Young Joe standing by WI home that later burned

Brothers Joe, Walter, and Frank in a Las Vegas hotel

Baby Lorraine, Joe, Rae, and hired help in Baker, CA

Rae and Joe in San Fernando, CA home

Tour Guide, Joe next to mother and family in Tijuana

Walter sharing nightly ritual with Joe in San Fernando

Family checking condition of copper kettle used in bootlegging in the 1920s

Joe and Margaret in the grotto of the Cathedral in the Desert near Grapevine Canyon

EPILOGUE

A Few Unopened Pages: Personal Glimpses

What goes into the making of a hero? Attorney William Perry Pendley, the author of *It Takes A Hero,* writes the stories of fifty-three outstanding men and women and identifies their characteristics. Although from many backgrounds, they all had certain things in common with Joe. They were heroes who has the courage to take on encroaching environmentalism and its millions of well funded political activists; heroes who challenged agents and agencies of the federal government and stood up to its bureaucrats, and its lawyers; heroes who were free thinkers and questioned political correctness; heroes who didn't wilt under criticism; heroes who started from nothing but their beliefs and determination; heroes whose actions continue to inspire others to reach high; heroes who are willing to sacrifice physical comforts for a higher purpose; who keep their heads under stress; keep a heart for fellow man; and always carry along an unquenchable sense of humor.

There are a couple of questions that demand an answer before the stories are complete. Why Joe? What made him into the hero? The answers come in bits and pieces as we catch glimpses of his early years and as we remember times that we spent with him.

Mother Louise and sons Eddie, Walter, Joe

Glimpse

Train up a child in the way he should go, and when he is old, he will not depart from it.

Proverbs 22:6 (KJV)

If child development studies are to be believed, then the personality of the man that Joe became was set by age four. The influence of his mother *produced the qualities of industriousness, inquisitiveness, clever inventiveness, perseverance, humor, and generosity.*

Louise Kolodziej came to the U.S., along with her widowed mother, as a three-year-old in the 1890s. It was Grandpa Golic who had arrived first and alone to settle on homestead land in Wisconsin. The pioneer life was extraordinarily labor-intense since the land was covered by virgin timber that needed to be cleared for cattle and for farming. Yet, he was soon able to pay for the passage of Louise and her mother, Mary.

Grandpa Golic had a generous loving nature and became the father figure and gentle teacher in this little girl's life. Louise lived through ninety-three difficult years of trials and testings. But what she had learned sitting on the lap of her precious grandpa carried her through each troubled year.

In her own words, she described her most cherished memories. "When I was little, I would sit on Grandpa's lap and he would read to me from his Bible. My mother never let me go to school, so I never learned to read or write. Grandpa was the only one who showed me a book or read to me."

Louise's most profound memory of her clever grandpa's resourcefulness was the unfortunate exchange that he had one day with the visiting circuit-riding priest. She could smile at the telling, but it was a day that had brought a rainstorm of tears from her young eyes.

The visit would have been welcome, but when the priest saw Grandpa's Bible, he scolded the good man and threw the book into the fire that was blazing in the cook stove. The priest was following a practice that had begun in the dark ages, and he proceeded to give a little sermon about illiterate Christians misinterpreting the Word of God.

The memory of that day was so clear to Louise that, despite her greatly advanced age, she remembered how her grandpa comforted her. After the priest left, Grandpa picked her up in his strong arms and said, "Don't worry, honey. I have another one over here." The Bible readings continued, and the little girl grew up to be the *post,* the stabilizing force of the family, in the harsh world of the nineteenth century.

There was a significant difference between the personality traits of Joe's mother, Louise, and Joe's father, Mike. Although Mike had the positive qualities of humor and generosity, he unfortunately also possessed generous doses of irresponsibleness, manipulativeness, restlessness, and addictiveness.

Mike had picked up one of his father's vices: the thirst for alcohol. But by standards of his day, Josef Ostre'ga was considered to be successful. Josef had provided well for his family in Poland. They were highly educated landowners who were able to hire servants. Josef had the foresight to plan to keep his sons, who were approaching draft age, from being drafted into that country's army. The sale of his property provided the funds to purchase passage to America for the entire family. Once in the Upper Michigan Peninsula, he bought land and built a small house.

The state was young and still being pioneered when Josef arrived with his family. This meant that it was a day's drive for a round-trip to the big city of Menominee where supplies were obtained. Out of necessity, there were many such drives as new buildings were to be added. It was on one such return trip, after loading his purchase of lumber, that this poor man's life ended abruptly. His habit of heavy drinking led to a disastrous horse-and-wagon accident.

Josef hadn't lived long enough to enjoy what this new country had to offer, but it was long enough to influence his son. The world that revolved around alcohol was the world that Mike chose to live in. This ended up being the world of the next generation: Joseph.

Growing up in that household, where hard work was the order of every day, Joe seemed to have been drawn to the carefreeness of Mike, his twinkly eyed, fiddle playing, hard drinking dad. Mike was a partier and just a bit of a wanderer. Although mistreated at the hands of his dad, Joe almost turned into a replica of Mike, both in looks and in personality type.

By God's good grace, there were also lessons learned from Mom that stuck. Joe had her inquiring mind and a strong will, which meant that he could accomplish whatever he set out to do. The lesson of salesmanship was the earliest and best remembered of all.

One of the family's nomadic experiences led them to Milwaukee. In order to supplement the income that often disappeared in a saloon, Louise used her clever inventiveness and developed a business plan. For the next several months, she purchased fish at the local fish market and sent her, three-, five-, and seven-year-old sons door to door selling fish from their little red wagon.

These appealing boys were such successful salesmen that Mike took over the business and the income while keeping his young boys busy pulling the wagon and selling fish. Never to be daunted, as the years went by, wherever they located Louise and the boys found new ways to raise money and stave off starvation. In their adult lives, Joe and his brothers used these lessons well.

Joe's inquisitiveness led to inventiveness and spilled over into everything that he did. It evidenced itself early when, at the age of ten or twelve, he put together a crystal radio, one of a rare few for the town of Oconto Falls. He had saved enough from his own earnings to send to a mail-order company for a radio kit and became the most popular fellow in the neighborhood.

Once he had left home, Joe's visits to Wisconsin were few. In the good old days, this meant that the visits were met with unusual festivities as brothers and sisters set their conservative lives on hold and prepared to celebrate in the old-fashioned, time-honored Polish ways.

Glimpse

I was eight years old when WWII ended. The brothers had all survived their tours of duty. That deserved a "victory celebration," and it took place at my parents' home. Sufficient amounts of alcohol were flowing to get someone high enough to leave footprints stamped on the walls and the ceilings. Fifty years later they were still laughing about the *wild enema bag chases.*

Glimpse

It was in the 1950s when Ike was president that my dad made a special trip "out West." Driving his oversized Chrysler sedan, he was able to bring along my mother, Margaret, her sister, Lucy, and Lucy's husband, Norman. Best of all, he had convinced his mother, Louise, to venture out with them.

This trip was a *first* for Joe's mother, and he and his wife, Rae, took great pains to provide her with the *grand tour.* Included in this tour was a border crossing into Mexico. The streets of Tijuana were lined with scores of Indian women and children along with Mexican merchants peddling their fascinating, sundry assortment of souvenirs. Colorful Mexican blankets were brought back to Wisconsin as reminders of this trip.

The whole experience could not be complete without some proper picture taking. The party happily donned sombreros and posed next to a burro. The next picture was taken at a Mexican cantina. Joe's mother never quite forgave him for that experience.

He couldn't resist a practical joke. This particular cantina not only served drinks, but also provided adult entertainment. It was a blushing mother who severely scolded her son and marched out of the cantina right after the nude dancers began to perform. Joe believed his practical joke was perfectly successful.

GLIMPSE

From my earliest years, I had learned to appreciate the kind, generous, fun-loving Joe from seeing him on his infrequent visits to Wisconsin. It was not until the mid 1960s that I was able to make what was my first visit to Joe's San Fernando, California, home. This was a family trip, and I was accompanied by my husband and children. While there, I observed that there was a lot more to this uncle than what I had expected. He was a complex, multi-dimensional man.

Joe and his wife, Rae, were skillful as host and hostess. They provided for every comfort and were entertaining, energetic tour guides. It was during this time that a few eccentricities also showed themselves and caught my attention.

TV was one example of a *Joe eccentricity*. When not in use, the TV was kept unplugged because Joe believed that it was a device that the government was using for spying purposes. Although he accepted the entertainment and news value of his TV, he never changed his mind about what he perceived was a threat to his privacy, nor did he change the habit of keeping the TV disconnected.

Whether the suspected bugging was true or not, Joe believed that it was a mistake to make assumptions or place blind faith in any government institution. He believed in a conspiracy theory that was aimed at interfering with this nation's civil rights and liberties.

Throughout his life, Joe remained a firm skeptic. He made great efforts to remain informed and vigilant. This led him to become an activist and outspoken supporter of the Miners' Union and Property Rights organizations among others.

Glimpse

Joe and Rae were extremely health-conscious. They were mainly vegetarians, and they were avid juicers. Yet, Joe's inordinate fondness for alcohol lasted all of his life. It was routine for Rae to join Joe every evening as he finished no less than a fifth of bourbon. Their cupboard was never dry, and there was always plenty of Mexican tequila, along with bottles of Jack Daniels and the like in their house.

Growing up in the age of Prohibition, he had every opportunity to lay hands on this clear, brown liquid at every turn. There was a bootleg still around every corner and, for a time, its sale was a good source of income for some family members.

Bootleg liquor was *big business* in Milwaukee from about 1919 to 1933. During the short time that Joe was living there, he would have seen the lively operation that was housed in his uncle's basement. The copper still probably produced enough high-quality alcohol to fill a dozen barrels that had been specially charred to give the brew its rich brown/amber glow.

The best customers came from the firehouse a couple of blocks away as well as from the local police department. These customers would receive delivery of gallon jugs of *high test* on a regular basis. In return, they gave advance warning if a raid was being planned.

On one occasion, the warning gave the date and included instructions. After removing the barrels to another location, they were to leave one jug in sight on the premises. When the house was raided, the jug was found and immediately broken, spilling its contents onto the cement floor. Joe's uncle was arrested, but his wife immediately bailed him out with $50, and they were in business again. It is known that Milwaukee's socialist mayor believed that Prohibition was a joke and stated so publicly.

In Joe's declining years, his evening alcohol consumption was reduced to one pint.

> In 1927, a speakeasy proprietor, whose premises were raided, sued the local precinct captain for breach of promise.
>
> —Tom Masson

> Prohibition helped to beautify American home life.
>
> It got rid of the rings around the bathtubs.
>
> —Gerald F. Lieberman

Glimpse

Mountains and deserts present challenges to survival even in the twenty-first century. One had to be desert-wise and physically hardy to know how to do this in the last century. There was no 911 number to call for travelers who had the misfortune of becoming sick or becoming incapacitated. If one should have an accident or run out of water, he stood a fair chance of meeting the *Grim Reaper.*

Joe's survival skills got him through until the day that he fell off the side of a mountain road while driving in his pickup. When this accident occurred, he was already in his sixties. His injuries left him half dead, and he lost track of the hours that he was trapped in the truck. If it were not for small miracles, his stories would have ended in that desolate place. But it seems that he still had things to do and places to go. He was found by someone passing through and shipped off to the nearest hospital to be mended. After several weeks of recovery, he was back in his beloved wilderness.

Glimpse

On one of our last trips to Nevada, Joe was given a special and most unorthodox tribute. My two sisters, Judy and Peg, had accompanied dad and myself on this particular visit. The idea for this tribute occurred as we were leaving. It may have included a little retaliation for the double-dare that he made as we were enjoying the inspiring Cathedral in the Desert.

The Cathedral is a privately owned natural grotto, a deep rock-walled depression in the middle of acres of barren Nevada landscape. A simple unpaved trail led us to the rim and wooden stairs spiraled their way down to the base of the grotto. Joe explained that the landowner had designed and decorated the walls to resemble a church in memory of a beloved daughter that had died. The surfaces on the irregular stone walls had niches that were laden with religious statuary, portraits, and biblical verses. A Guest Book was placed where visitors, who found their way to the grotto, could leave their names. Many had left notes giving thanks for answered prayers or notes requesting prayer. A miniature Christ of the Andes was placed at the top of a stairway that leads into the small canyon. Joe dared the girls to cross the canyon on its dilapidated and very unkempt swinging bridge. No one would take the dare as he was standing in the middle of the bridge, jumping up and down and laughing heartily.

At the end of what had been one of our best-guided tours of all, we reluctantly had to take our leave and return home. As we were dropping off the rental car outside of the airport in Las Vegas, there were no words to express our mixed emotions. Joe had been a gleeful companion showing us the desert sites and more of Las Vegas. Good-byes can be sad and awkward, but we determined that it would not be so—not this time. Much to his surprise, he was lifted up by his nieces and was made to stand on a cement bench right there on the sidewalk. Grinning from ear to ear, he listened to a somewhat out of tune and very public rendition of "For He's a Jolly Good Fellow."

Had that happy, carefree moment lasted a little longer, we would say this trip had a happy ending. But, there are foibles to foul even the best of times.

Shortly after arriving at home, we received a letter from Joe. In it, he mentioned that he was briefly left stranded at the car rental because he had tried to leave their lot using the wrong lane. Trying to exit on the lane marked *Entrance* meant running over metal strips that shredded his tires. After having had such an enjoyable visit, we were more than happy to pick up the cost of those tires and would not accept his refusal.

There are bits and pieces set aside, in little displays, as reminders of Joe. So many times, his generosity would spill over as he would choose mementos to send home with us. We remember his days as a businessman in Baker when we pick up the few ivory and pink, ceramic, one-inch tiles that had been part of the floor in his restaurant.

When we study the varieties of ore that came from some of his mines, we remember his days as a prospector. There are almost eighty years of photos, some dating back to his childhood, that help in the remembering. Though he is no longer there, we remember the sight of the work shed that sat behind his home in Pahrump, as well as his assaying equipment and machinery.

Over the years, Joe had hit the heights and dropped to the depths only to rise up again just like the hills and valleys he had explored. His life was a race that wasn't just about the winning. It was about finishing and about how well he ran. How he enjoyed the race!

May those who read the record of his exploits have as much thirst for learning, hunger for discovery, and courage of their convictions as he had.

From this written record and from photos taken over the years, we will remember the stories.

REFERENCES

Baker Valley News, Sept 16, 1994. Story by Lois Clark

Orange County Register, Sept 25, 1994 *"Myth of The Fragile Desert"* by Don Fife

Pahrump Valley Gazette, Aug. 29, 1996. Story by Doug McMurdo

International California Mining Journal, June, 1996 *"Desert Closure Act (S.21)" Shuts Down World Class Wollastonite Mine* by Don L. Fife of the National Assoc. of Mining Districts and American Land Rights Assoc.

The American Oil & Gas Reporter", April 1997 Vol. 40 No. 4 *Law Gone Loco* by Don Fife

The Leader, Lucerne Valley's Community Newspaper Nov 6, 2002 *"Everybody Knows They're Not Really Endangered: We just need them to stop mining,* by Don Fife

The Professional Geologist, March 2001, *Instant Wilderness: When a Road is not a Road* by Don Fife and Ralph Pray, National Assoc. of Mining Districts

Media Release: *Environmental Hysteria Can Kill*, by Don Fife, National Assoc. of Mining Districts. Don Fife also appears in the televised documentary produced by CBN on the 700 Club titled *War On The West.*

Joe Ostringer, taped interview for TV Special Documentary produced by CBN on the 700 Club titled, *War On The West*

Fact Sheet called *The Wild West–Grassroots Battle Over Public Lands.* Phone 1–800–716-FACT for free copies.

Death Valley, Splendid Isolation, by Stewart Aitchinson

It Takes A Hero: The Grassroots Battle Against

Environmental Oppression, by Wm. Perry Pendley

War on the West: Government Tyranny on America's Great Frontier, by Wm Perry Pendley

The Coming Breakpoint, by Barry Goldwater

Pattern of Deception, by Tim Graham

The New Scofield Reference Bible

Personal hand written letters from Don Fife to Jane Delveaux, June 25, 2008

WEBSITES

www.sovereignty.net

www.takingliberty.us

www.uneswco.org//mab/the Mabnet.html

www.eagleforum.org/topics/global/global.html

www.circleID.com/posts/
un_global_forum_on_internet_governance/

www.apfn.org/apfn/global/governance.htm

www.trilateral.org

www.environmentalgovernance.org

www.globalresearch.ca/articles/

www.eoearth.org

www.un.org/issues/m-gov.html

www.americanpolicycenter.ort/un/
globalgoverness. htm

www.conspiracyarchive.com/NWO/
Global/Governess/1.htmm

www.mayaruins.com

www.sanclemente.com/ole_hanson.phpp

www.en.wikipedia.org/wiki/moe.dalitz

www.nps.gov/history/history/online
books/deva/section3a14htm

www.palomar.edu/geology/DVweb.htm

www.terragalleria.com/parks/np.death-valley.all.html

www.geopen.com/samples/vh.goldincentralamerica.pdf